MIMI AND
THE BISCUIT FACTORY

VIVECA SUNDVALL

PICTURES BY
EVA ERIKSSON

TRANSLATED BY ERIC BIBB

R&S
BOOKS

Stockholm   New York   London   Toronto   Adelaide

E
SYN

Rabén & Sjögren Stockholm

Translation copyright © 1989 by Eric Bibb
All rights reserved
Illustrations copyright © 1988 by Eva Eriksson
Originally published in Sweden by Rabén & Sjögren
under the title *Mimmi och kexfabriken,*
text copyright © 1988 by Viveca Sundvall
Library of Congress catalog card number: 88-26318
Printed in Denmark
First edition, 1989

ISBN 91 29 59142 2

R & S Books are distributed in the United States of America
by Farrar, Straus and Giroux, New York;
in the United Kingdom by Ragged Bears, Andover;
in Canada by General Publishing, Toronto;
and in Australia by ERA Publications, Adelaide

90-13576

I live in a yellow house in a small town in Sweden. My name is Mimi Lindström. My dad has a mustache and his name is Oskar. He's a mailman. My mom's name is Helen, and she's a waitress at the Golden Swan.

The Golden Swan

Sometimes, when she's working evenings, Dad and I stand
out on the balcony. We can see a lot of lights from up there,
and when we sniff the air, we can smell Henry's bread and
biscuit factory down by the river. They make a million
biscuits a day. Everyone in our town loves Henry's biscuits,
except Sven Olsson, who's allergic to them. That's what
Albert told me.

Albert goes to the same school as me, and he's six years old,
like me. But he's not a girl like me. Even so, I like him. He can
count up to 42.
Albert's dad owns the whole town. That's what Albert says.
And in the evenings he plays darts with Sven Olsson, who's
allergic to Henry's biscuits.

Our teacher has promised that one day she'll take all eighteen
of us to see Henry's Bread and Biscuits.
Then we'll each get our own bag of old, broken biscuits.
I can't wait for that day.
I also can't wait for the day when I get a loose tooth.

We went to Henry's bakery at the end of May.
It was a Monday.
Dad made breakfast and ate it in a big hurry, so he wouldn't
be late for work.
Just as he was getting up from the table and brushing the
crumbs from his mustache, I screamed as loud as I could.

I had discovered that one of my baby teeth had become
extremely wobbly.
Dad was happy, too. Before he left, he turned on the radio,
so I could wiggle my tooth in time to the music.
I was so happy!

Albert and the other children and our teacher were already
waiting outside the school when I came running.
"I've got a loose tooth, Albert!" I shouted.
Jane copied me: "I've got a loose tooth, Albert!" she squealed
four times in a silly voice.

We walked in line down to Henry's Bread and Biscuits, and I
wiggled my tooth almost the whole time.
Albert walked beside me, and the sun was shining on us both.

When we came to the factory, we had to pass a guard who sat in a little booth. He didn't look very happy. But inside the gates we met a guide named Greta, and in the beginning she was in a really good mood. She gave everyone a cap that said Henry's Bread and Biscuits.

The guide said we would see a movie about the
factory, since we weren't allowed to walk
around all the tools, the dough, and the
machines.
"Is it a Donald Duck movie?" asked Albert.
The guide didn't answer.
"They speak Swedish in the movie, right?" I
asked.
"Quiet!" she shouted.

The movie was very boring. It was about Henry's father, who started Henry's Bread and Biscuits. Albert lay down on the floor and went to sleep right away. At least I had my tooth to wiggle.

Then we got to walk around the factory a little and look at the huge tubs with dough in them. I was leaning over one of them, when Albert said: "Don't drop your tooth in the dough." I got very scared. When you lose a tooth, you have to put it in a glass of water so that it turns into a quarter.
"If the tooth gets into a bun and they sell the bun in the store to some guy and he finds the tooth, well, Mimi's tooth will get into the newspapers . . ." said Albert.

"Quiet now. Here comes Henry himself," said
the guide.
Henry was wearing a white coat, and his cheeks
were fat and pink.
He asked us if we had any questions.

"Will our cheeks get as fat and pink as yours if we eat your biscuits?" I asked.

My teacher and the guide stared at me. Then they both smiled at Henry. It got very quiet.

"But I think pink cheeks look nice," I said.

"I think so, too, little friend," said Henry.

The two ladies sighed with relief.

"I eat eighty-six biscuits a day," said Henry.
"Everybody should. The recipe for Henry's biscuits is secret.
My father made it up, and he whispered it into my ear before
he died. Before I die, I'll whisper it into Rosamunda's ear."
"Is that a cow?" asked Albert.

The teacher and the guide groaned.
"It could very well be," said Henry calmly.
"In this case, it happens to be my daughter. She'll be taking
over the factory one day."
"But if you're out biking without a helmet and get run over,
then you won't have time to whisper the recipe," said Jane.
"Actually, I drive a Mercedes," said Henry.

By now Albert had been standing for so long that
he just had to shout:
"My stomach is dead from Henry's bread.
If you dare to risk it, try a biscuit."
That's a funny rhyme he learned from Sven Olsson, who
works at the factory and is allergic to biscuits.

Albert called out his dead–stomach rhyme at least
thirty-four times. Nothing happened.

Then I shouted it once, in a tiny voice.
That's when Henry shouted:
"Be quiet, child!"

After that, we each got a bag of old, broken biscuits and a fresh bun to take home.

Outside the factory gates I bit into the bun, and my loose tooth got stuck in it. The bun got a little blood on it, and almost all the children fainted on the sidewalk. I stuffed the tooth bun in my pocket, and when I got home, I put the whole thing in a big glass of water.

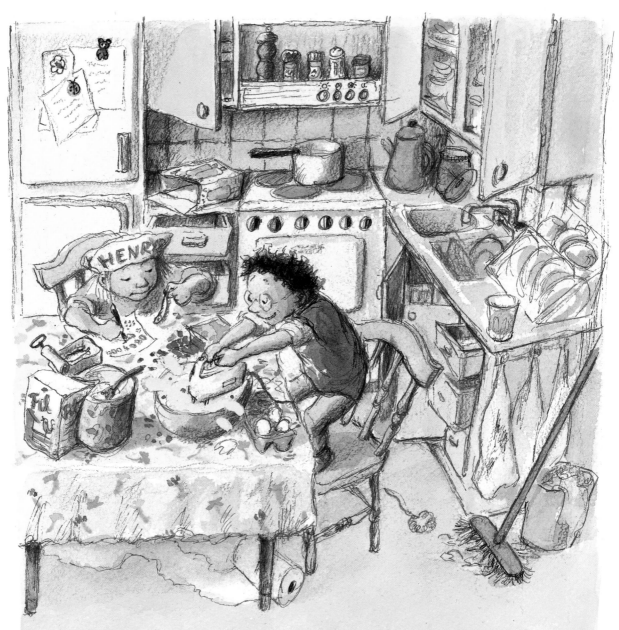

Then I forgot about it because Albert and I locked ourselves
in the kitchen to invent a secret recipe.
We made a wonderful dough and wrote down all the
ingredients on a piece of paper. Since we're not very good at
writing, we drew pictures instead.
Here's our secret recipe: 9 cornflakes, 8 tablespoons butter-
milk, 16 raisins, 8 eggs, half a can of sardines, and 4 melted ice
creams (the kind on a stick).

Then we took our recipe and snuck out to an old brick wall, where we hid it. We're going to get it out in twenty years.

We ate a little bit of what we had
baked, and then I went straight to
bed. It's hard to be in a factory.
I woke at the sound of a pling.
It was my tooth that had turned
into a quarter in the glass. The bun
was also gone.

With my quarter I bought a green pear.

90-13576

E   Sundvall, Viveca
SUN
         Mimi and the
           biscuit factory

$12.95

DATE			
West			